Selected Poem

CHARLOTTE MEW was born in London in 186
tect, and was educated at a London girls' scho
was a short story in *The Yellow Book* in 1894. Living in difficult circum-stances with her mother and sister Anne, an artist, Mew found a measure of freedom from isolation and failed relationships, notably with the novelist May Sinclair, in holidays in France and Belgium. In the years from 1913 she became increasingly productive as a poet: her first collec-tion, *The Farmer's Bride*, was published in 1916, to be followed by a larger edition in 1921, and a second collection *The Rambling Sailor* in 1929. In 1923 she was awarded a Civil List pension on the recommendation of John Masefield, Walter de la Mare and Thomas Hardy. In 1927, still grieving from the death of her sister, Mew killed herself.

EAVAN BOLAND was born in Dublin. Her first book was published in 1967; Carcanet publish her eight poetry collections, her prose book *Object Lessons* and her *New Collected Poems* (2005). She has received numerous awards for her writing. She is Mabury Knapp Professor at Stanford University where she is director of the Creative Writing Program. She divides her time between California and Dublin where she lives with her husband, the novelist Kevin Casey.

FyfieldBooks aim to make available some of the great classics of British and European literature in clear, affordable formats, and to restore often neglected writers to their place in literary tradition.

FyfieldBooks take their name from the Fyfield elm in Matthew Arnold's 'Scholar Gypsy' and 'Thyrsis'. The tree stood not far from the village where the series was originally devised in 1971.

Roam on! The light we sought is shining still.
Dost thou ask proof? Our tree yet crowns the hill,
Our Scholar travels yet the loved hill-side

from 'Thyrsis'

CHARLOTTE MEW

Selected Poems

Edited with an introduction by
EAVAN BOLAND

FyfieldBooks

CARCANET

First published in Great Britain in 2008 by
Carcanet Press Limited
Alliance House
Cross Street
Manchester M2 7AQ

A CIP catalogue record for this book is available from the British Library
ISBN 978 1 85754 962 1

The publisher acknowledges financial assistance from Arts Council England

Typeset by XL Publishing Services, Tiverton
Printed and bound in England by SRP Ltd, Exeter

Contents

Introduction

Charlotte Mew was born in London in 1869. Her family – middle-class, respectable, afflicted – lived at number 30 Doughty Street in the borough of Camden. I lived near there as a child in the 1950s, when the airy squares with their chestnut and plane trees, their white wedding cake houses, were still almost intact.

By that time however, London was pitted and humbled by two wars. To find Charlotte Mew's city we have to peel back the erosion, the doubt, the fog-scars of a hundred years until we come to a place that glows with empire. Pepys's London. The London of the novelists. A few houses down, nearer to Russell Square, Charles Dickens had written his early novels at number 48. What more could a child like Charlotte Mew want, you might ask, than to be born in the environs of a luminous gossip and a great novelist?

The census of 4 April 1881 suggests a normal Victorian family with their children: Henry H. Mew, aged fifteen, Scholar, Charlotte M. Mew, aged eleven, Scholar, Caroline F.A. Mew, aged seven and Freda K. Mew aged two, together with the live-in servants: Elizabeth Goodman, aged fifty-six, 'Nurse Domestic', and Lucy Best, aged eighteen, 'Cook Domestic'.

But appearances, here as elsewhere, can be deceptive. A more vulnerable and struggling family would be hard to find. The terrible story begins early. One child died. Two more died when Charlotte was seven, one of fever, the other of convulsions. Her only brother, Henry, became schizophrenic early in life. And her youngest sister, Freda, notable in that homely family for being 'beautiful as a flame', became schizophrenic at sixteen. It must all have bewildered Frederick Mew, Charlotte's father. He was an architect, but not a particularly enterprising one. His wife, the daughter of a more eminent architect, had social and financial expectations he failed to fulfil. Fred Mew's income did not increase. But his family did. By 1879 there were seven children. The shadows were growing longer.

Death. Insanity. Class. Suddenly, in that apparent decorum of imperial England, a window opens into a savage time. The Mew family are the dark side of empire. Charlotte Mew lived the pain and contradiction: the shame of a genteel life lived without the money gentility requires; the pain of a sexuality gentility would reject.

Charlotte Mew's childhood might have remained hidden but for one stray account. In 1913 she published an essay in the *New Statesman* called 'The Old Servant'. It is a strange prose – staccato and choked with memory – but it reveals one of the formative relations of her life.

Mew's grandmother, Mary Cobham Kendall, had not approved of her daughter's marriage to the weak and unsuitable Fred Mew. Faced with the fact, however, she selected a servant from her own household to help her. Elizabeth Goodman, tall, spare, a blunt North countrywoman, came to that house to practise the arts of survival: cuff-mending and darning, the skilful turning of sheets. And the less visible arts of unseen friendship.

Of all the photographs of Charlotte Mew, this may be the most compelling: Two women, neatly dressed in dark clothes, sit in a Victorian conservatory. The younger, who has no hat or bonnet on as the older one does, leans forward slightly as if she could see or hear something. More likely, the photographer has told them both to look into the middle distance. The young woman has short, unstyled hair. Her face is a strange oval. It is neither pretty nor usual, but intense and already odd. The older woman – almost an old woman – wears the dark cloak and bonnet of a nineteenth-century domestic. She is sitting to the front of the picture. The young woman stands behind her shoulder like a dark spirit, a familiar. It is a stern portrait. But for all that, this is a photograph of one of the few friendships, the few unflawed empathies of Mew's life. The ramrod straight woman brought a magic to her childhood, all the deeper because it addressed the Puritan nature of both. 'Throughout the year her reading was limited to the Bible,' Mew writes,

> and a cheap weekly comic paper; but on Christmas eve she flung into the festooned disorder of the nursery a pile of Christmas numbers and thenceforth walked with us, for a week or two, in the world of pure romance. Red lights gleamed from Manor House windows; ostlers bandied jests in the courtyards of lonely inns; the crack of whips and the hoofs of post-horses drowned the wheels of the crawling cab and the bell of the muffin man ting-tinging down our long, dull street.

Despite these brief moments, it was an outsider's childhood. In a piece she wrote called 'An Open Door', Mew recalls, 'As a child, I remember looking down from our high nursery windows on the children, far below us under the railings of the park.' Her way of being at the side of an action would last her whole life and painfully enrich her work. Now that life would begin in earnest: in 1879 she was entered as a pupil at the Gower Street School in London.

In 1888 the family moved to Gordon Street, to a larger, more expensive and far more unlucky house. There, within the space of four years, two of the children drifted into insanity. Henry, Charlotte's only brother, was confined to hospital in his early twenties and never re-emerged. His death certificate of March 1901 lists the place of death as Peckham House Lunatic Asylum. He is said to be buried in Nunhead Cemetery. Freda, the beautiful youngest girl, followed him in her late teens. Alida Monro, a later friend of Mew, opened a small window into the events when she commented, 'Their sad condition was a constant torment to Charlotte.'

* * *

The startling, off-kilter poems published when she was nearly fifty years of age in her first book, *The Farmer's Bride*, gather and filter the tragedies of Charlotte Mew's youth. They have an eerie verve, these poems. Their conversational staccato, played off the truncated cadences of Victorian lyric, gives a studio acoustic to the voice. The voice – and this is unusual in that era – signals from its margins and its music through tone. The combination of the two tells us something we can hardly ignore:

No year has been like this that has just gone by;
    It may be that what Father says is true,
If things are so it does not matter why:
    But everything is burned and not quite through.
    The colours of the world have turned
    To flame, to blue, the gold has burned
In what used to be such a leaden sky.
When you are burned quite through you die.

The reader has to look closely here so as not to miss the effect. Mew is not a lyric poet. At least, not a conventional one – and certainly not in that era of lyric poets. She is something different and far more unexpected in a time when there was still honey for tea: she is a pre-modernist narrator, gathering her world into lines which tumble off the edge of the page with the strain of holding it together. Cemeteries, asylums, sea roads and broken dolls clutter these lines. The cast of characters is strange and estranged. While the Georgian poets of that era were seeking out small pastorals, she marked a disharmony. She stands in the middle of her Edwardian landscape, not to be framed by it, but to signal its danger, like a fire-swallower at an otherwise sedate country fair.

These qualities did not guarantee a literary welcome. Mew received little recognition in her lifetime. The full chill of neglect can be felt in the lines in a local newspaper noticing her death. Even the name is wrong. She is described as 'Charlotte New, said to be a writer'. The earlier years were no better. She was not included in Edward Marsh's 1910 volume *Georgian Poetry*.

And then there is the issue of both gender and sexuality – neither overtly disclosed in the poems, but nevertheless the weather of many of them. Mew's sexuality is at once secretive and hiding in plain sight. It discloses itself, not as actions or partnerships, but as subtle obsessions of light and view; transgressions of feeling, as in 'On the Road to the Sea' where she imagines the childhood of the person she fantasises about. The lines are not comfortable, but they are – as is so much in Mew – luminously arresting:

> Now, if I look, I see you walking down the years,
> Young, and through August fields – a face, a thought, a swinging
> dream perched on a stile – ;
> I would have liked (so vile we are!) to have taught you tears

In 1894 Mew's short story 'Passed' was published in the second issue of *The Yellow Book*. It was her first publication; she was twenty-five. It is also one of the few available records of her youth. She wrote copious prose. Most of it is worthy; little is excellent. She wrote in a stiff essay-dialect entirely missing from her poems. And, in any case, none of it offers much information.

In fact, trying to pick up her trail as a young woman is frustrating. It would be almost impossible without some essays and introductions and information. Above all there is Penelope Fitzgerald's splendid and affectionate book *Charlotte Mew and Her Friends*, with its fine preface by Brad Leithauser. And, of course, Val Warner's essential, meticulous editing of *Collected Poems and Prose*. There is also the rich, detailed and fascinating Middlesex University website 'Charlotte's Web' (www.mdx.ac.uk/WWW/STUDY/xmew.htm). Out of some of these accounts, a few details gleam.

Here, for instance, is Charlotte Mew asking Henry Harland, the editor of *The Yellow Book* to pay her all at once for 'Passed'. Here she is falling in love with his secretary, Ella D'Arcy who leaves London to live in the Channel Islands. There she is, just out of reach of her friends, rolling her own cigarettes, swearing forcefully, and dressing in darker and more masculine clothes by the day. And here she is again – with the cold ring of truth – writing about Emily Brontë for the journal *Temple Bar* in 1904. It is a short essay. But there at the top of a page one sentence comes to life and turns its prophetic head. It turns and looks back at the fragile, desolate young woman who wrote it: 'Her nature stood alone', she writes of Brontë: 'That was the awful fact – the tragedy of her life.'

We are coming to that part of Mew's story which shows her at her most abandoned. Hers was a life of terrible loneliness. It was not simply that she was lesbian in a time of repression and restriction. There is also her social personality. She was a strange and volatile mix of attributes: she had a fierce, structured religious faith. It connected her to a visionary sense of order. It also dissociated her from the body. In the best of Mew's poetry these contradictions play off each other: there is an off-kilter fervour about her eroticism, and an erotic yearning to her spiritual world. It is a beautiful, heart-rending blend.

Nevertheless, in a plain and poignant sense, she found little peace or renewal within her sexuality. She made a series of approaches and received a series of agonising rebuffs. She went from London to Paris in 1902 to join Ella D'Arcy, the former secretary to Henry Harland of *The Yellow Book*. She was excited, hopeful, tentative. But Ella D'Arcy was a heterosexual and Mew shrank back in humiliation. Years later, the same thing would happen in her relations with May Sinclair – an ardent affection would be turned back. In that case it was more public and still more humiliating. In fact, one of Sinclair's friends noted with asperity in her diary 'Charlotte is a pervert'. In Mew's own poignant phrase she had 'made herself dam ridiculous'.

It was obvious she was looking for freedom and experiment, as well as an intellectual acceptance of her own sexuality. But in that closed era it eluded her. The peace of the body was not to be found. There is a grim loneliness to the erotic undersong in many of the poems. It would make for bleak reading, if the music of tone and voice were not so unswerving. Nevertheless the story of Mew's agonising, hidden life has to be imagined because it is so much the hinterland of her poems. We have to imagine the rented rooms and seaside hotels and friends' houses in which she received the rejections which must have terrified her. But if she lost her sense of sexual dignity there she also found, in that ordeal, one of her most luminous poems:

> I remember rooms that have had their part
>   In the steady slowing down of the heart.
> The room in Paris, the room at Geneva
> The little damp room with the seaweed smell,

And that ceaseless, maddening sound of the tide
    Rooms where for good or ill things died.

And here the story is taken up by Alida Monro, who writes a biographical memoir to the beautiful, small 1953 edition of Mew's *Collected Poems*. I own that book; it is a talisman of mine. I keep it near me, always knowing that within its rosy, tattered dustjacket and sturdy covers burns and lives the music of dissidence.

In 1915 Mew was invited to the Poetry Bookshop on the Strand, owned by Alida Monro's husband. Through the door came a tiny, strange woman, not more than four foot ten inches. 'Her face was a fine oval', writes Monro 'and she always wore a little, hard pork-pie hat put on very straight.' On that first occasion, Monro asked her if she was Charlotte Mew. She replied with a smile, saying 'I am sorry to say I am.'

Mew was nearly fifty when her first book, *The Farmer's Bride*, was published by Harold Monro's press. The year was 1916. It came out as a chapbook, in a coarse, gunmetal-coloured jacket. The cover shows a child's drawing of a house. The roof slopes towards two small windows. A pair of fork-sharp trees are behind it. Next to the logo of 'The Poetry Bookshop' is the inky symbol of a shilling.

It remains one of the most remarkable poetry publications of the first half of the twentieth century. The edition of 1916 contains just seventeen poems. Some of them – 'In Nunhead Cemetery', 'The Farmer's Bride', 'Madeleine in Church' – are signature Mew poems. Others are shorter. Most have her bleak strength. In 1921 the volume was re-issued with eleven new poems, keeping its name in Britain, but titled *Saturday Market* in the United States. Much later, not until 1953, the *Collected Poems* was published in both countries.

In fact, there are two stories folded into Mew's book, one visible and the other hidden. The first is of a compelling, lapsed lyric poet, a writer of harsh lines and scalding images, who sought out – unusually in a time of Georgian sentiment – Hardy's darkness and offered herself as its inheritrix. Mew wrote an odd line: long and wayward, and far more voice – driven than was common in that era:

Do you remember the two old people we passed on the road to Kérity,
Resting their sack on the stones, by the drenched wayside,

In the spirit of Hardy, her best poems show her ability to write a lurid pastoral. Not the quiet celebration of England from a Victorian instruction set, but poems furnished with madhouses, broken spirits, unrecoverable partings. And yet her poems can also have an ominous pre-Auden elegance of tone:

When we were children old Nurse used to say,
    The house was like an auction or a fair
Until the lot of us were safe in bed.
It has been quiet as the country-side
Since Ted and Janey and then Mother died
And Tom crossed Father and was sent away.

But it is together, rather than singly, that the poems in this book open out into the second story – the one which is less visible, the one which helps to make Mew such an essential figure.

* * *

The nineteenth century was a time of sinister enchantment for women poets. As if by sorcery, they ceased to be poets and became 'poetesses'. One by one, Rossetti, Browning, and even Emily Brontë (at least in her poems) surrendered to a limiting sub-category: one designed by an anxious Empire to reconcile acts of imagination with the obedience normally required of daughters and wives. During their courtship, Elizabeth Barrett wrote to Robert Browning:

> Thus you have an immense grasp in Art; and no one at all accustomed to consider the usual forms of it could help regarding with reverence and gladness the gradual expansion of your powers. Then you are 'masculine' to the height – and I, as a woman, have studied some of your gestures of language and intonation wistfully, as a thing beyond me far! and the more admirable for being beyond.

A sinister enchantment? The term is hardly too harsh. When Elizabeth Barrett wrote in one of her first letters to Robert Browning that her spirits drooped to the ground 'like an untrained honeysuckle', she provided the quintessential image of the poetess. But it was more than social expectation. The subtle, continuous, offset and interplay all through the nineteenth century of expectations of the poetess led directly to the lyric of religious yearning, of disappointed love, and sacred surrender: the four-stress, eight-beat line of an obedient music.

Then the break came. But how? By any logic, only a woman poet so estranged from the society which made the category could begin to dismantle its expectation of the poetess. Charlotte Mew fits that description. So dissident, so lost, so out on a margin of voice, craft and canon – ironically, she possessed, in all her powerlessness, the requisite power: she could prove the category deficient. And she did. The great unshackling of women's voices in poetry has one of its beginnings right here. These sad, beautiful poems are full of rendings and breakings and burnings.

Charlotte Mew lived for twelve more years after *The Farmer's Bride*. In the spring of 1928, after the death of her sister, she entered a nursing home in Beaumont Street. She stayed there, in a shuttered, plain room for weeks. In March, at the threshold of spring, she left the house on a Saturday morning to make a purchase. She bought a bottle of Lysol – a creosote mixture – and drank a small glass of it. She died, foaming at the mouth, a few hours later. There is no bleaker death in the history of poetry.

* * *

I have wanted this book to be an introduction. Just that. There is a sort of salt and spray about reading Mew for the first time: her poems are not like anything else. No reading of Victorian or Edwardian poetry prepares for them. If the big, wilful lines, the direct voice, seem like transgressions, it is because they are. They have enough force to unwrite the false pastorals of Georgian England and the dead sweetness of pre-modernist, post-Victorian poetry.

Mew built her poems in a radical and prescient way. She had little imaginative loyalty to narrative traditions or lyric inheritance. She was a maverick with rhetorical strategies. A poem like 'On the Road to the Sea' – which is typical of her longer work – begins with a suppressed narrative, moves quickly to a lyric sketch of childhood and back to a darker mix of both. In this way, a portrait of erotic obsession is rescued from a conventional framework. Mew is not a modernist. But she has an acute sense of how to set up an alliance with fragmentation. She is a headstrong and wonderful technician.

For these and other reasons, the selection here has not been hard. Mew is not always consistent. There are some slight poems; some weak ones, too. They may be interesting for the scholar of Mew's work, but not for an introduction to it. It has not been difficult, therefore, to decide on which heady anti-pastorals to choose; scenarios of an England no one knew existed: 'The Farmer's Bride', for instance, with its disappointments and its final grace; 'In Nunhead Cemetery', with its desolate hinterland; 'On the Road to the Sea', one of the strongest accounts of sexual malaise that era produced; 'Peri on mer', with its early music of elegy. There are also the short poems – 'Rooms', 'À quoi bon dire', with their wonderful sleight of hand in tone and rhyme. I have included these – although there are missing favourites too – while trying to imagine their startling and powerful effect on a new reader. In a sense, I envy that reader. I found Mew's work in my thirties – a poem here and there. Its effect was gradual, not sudden. I wished then, as I do now, that I had found it in some compact and available form when I was a beginning poet. Its courage and plain-spoken syntax would certainly have shaped me. But I didn't read those poems at a formative moment. I hope that the new reader will. I can, in fact, imagine the effect. Fortunately, I don't need to find words for it. The description of how these poems reach their audience is already there in Mew's essay on Brontë. 'When first we read these songs,' she writes, all the way back in 1904, 'we are brought face to face with the woman who wrote them. And when once we know them and have been haunted by their rebellious and contending music it will not be possible to forget.'

Eavan Boland,
Dublin 2007

Chronology

1868 Born at 30 Doughty Street, London, third child of Frederick and Anna Mew, two years after the death at seven months of Frederick Mew, her brother.

1871 Birth of brother, Richard Cobham Mew.

1873 Birth of (Caroline Frances) Anne Mew, sister.

1875 Birth of Daniel Kendall Mew, brother.

1876 Death of Christopher Barnes Mew (brother) at four months.

1876 Death of Richard Cobham Mew, at five years, of scarlet fever.

1879 Enrolled in the Lucy Harrison's School for Girls in Gower Street. Birth of Freda Kendall Mew, sister.

1888 Anne Mew enters the Female School of Art in Queen's Square. The Mews move from Doughty Street to 9 Gordon Street, Gordon Square, Bloomsbury.

1891 Charlotte Mew gets ticket to the British Museum Reading Room, used until 1927.

1894 First publication of fiction – 'Passed' – published in July, in second issue of *The Yellow Book*.

1895 Finishes long story 'The China Bowl', which is rejected by *The Yellow Book*.

1898 'F.K.M.' (Freda Mew, sister) listed as patient in Isle of Wight County Lunatic Asylum.

1898 Death of Frederick Mew, father.

1899 Essay 'The Governess in Fiction' published in *The Academy*.

1901 Death of Henry Herne Mew, brother, at Peckham House Lunatic Asylum, Surrey. By repute, buried in Nunhead Cemetery. Essay 'Miss Bolt' published in *Temple Bar*. Travels to Brittany with five women companions. Poem 'To a Little Child in Death' published in *Temple Bar*.

1902 Stays in Paris for summer at 26 Rue de Turin.

1904 Essay on Emily Brontë published in *Temple Bar*.

1909 Visits Brittany during summer.

1911 Visits Boulogne.

1912 Poem 'The Farmer's Bride' published in *The Nation*. Meets Sappho Dawson Scott, hostess and later founder of International P.E.N.

1913 Meets May Sinclair, popular British novelist. Takes a writing holiday in Dieppe.

Harold Monro opens The Poetry Bookshop at Devonshire Street, London.

1915 Meets Alida and Harold Monro.

1916 Publication in May of *The Farmer's Bride* by The Poetry Bookshop.

1921 New edition of *The Farmer's Bride* published, with eleven new poems. Published in the United States by Macmillan with the title *Saturday Market*.

Louis Untermeyer reviews *Saturday Market* in *New York Evening Post*.

1922 Charlotte Mew, her mother and sister, move from Gordon Street to 86 Delancey Street, Camden Town.

1923 Death of Anna Maria Mew, mother.

1924 National Portrait Gallery buys Dorothy Hawkesley portrait of Charlotte Mew.

1927 Horatio Cowan, Fitzroy Square, begins to treat Charlotte Mew for depression.

Anne Mew, sister and companion, dies in June of cancer at 53.

1928 In February enters nursing home in Beaumont Street for 'neurasthenia'.

Charlotte Mew commits suicide on 24 March, by drinking Lysol.

Buried beside Anne in Hampstead Cemetery, Fortune Green Road.

The Farmer's Bride

Three Summers since I chose a maid,
Too young maybe – but more's to do
At harvest-time that a bide and woo.
   When us was wed she turned afraid
Of love and me and all things human;
Like the shut of winter's day
Her smile went out, and 'twasn't a woman –
   More like a little frightened fay.
      One night, in the Fall, she runned away.

'Out 'mong the sheep, her be,' they said,
Should properly have been abed;
But sure enough she wasn't there
Lying awake with her wide brown stare.
   So over seven-acre field and up-along across the down
We chased her, flying like a hare
Before out lanterns. To Church-Town
   All in a shiver and a scare
We caught her, fetched her home at last
   And turned the key upon her, fast.

She does the work about the house
As well as most, but like a mouse:
   Happy enough to chat and play
   With birds and rabbits and such as they,
   So long as men-folk keep away
'Not near, not near!' her eyes beseech
When one of us comes within reach.
   The woman say that beasts in stall
   Look round like children at her call.
   I've hardly heard her speak at all.

Shy as a leveret, swift as he,
Straight and slight as a young larch tree,
Sweet as the first wild violets, she,
To her wild self. But what to me?

The short days shorten and the oaks are brown,
　　The blue smoke rises to the low grey sky,
One leaf in the still air falls slowly down,
　　A magpie's spotted feathers lie
On the black earth spread white with rime,
The berries redden up to Christmas-time.
　　What's Christmas-time without there be
　　Some other in the house than we!

　　She sleeps up in the attic there
　　Alone, poor maid. 'Tis but a stair
Betwixt us. Oh! my God! the down,
　　The soft young down of her, the brown,
The brown of her – her eyes, her hair, her hair!

On the Asylum Road

Theirs is the house whose windows – every pane –
  Are made of darkly stained or clouded glass:
Sometimes you come upon them in the lane,
  The saddest crowd that you will ever pass.

But still we merry town or village folk
  Throw to their scattered stare a kindly grin,
And think no shame to stop and crack a joke
  With the incarnate wages of man's sin.

None but ourselves in our long gallery we meet,
  The moor-hen stepping from her reeds with dainty feet,
    The hare-bell bowing on its stem,
Dance not with us; their pulses beat
  To fainter music; nor do we to them
    Make their life sweet.

The gayest crowd that they will ever pass
  Are we to brother-shadows in the lane:
Our windows, too, are clouded glass
  To them, yes, every pane!

In the Fields

Lord when I look at lovely things which pass,
  Under old trees the shadows of young leaves
Dancing to please the wind along the grass,
  Or the gold stillness of the August sun on the August sheaves;
Can I believe there is a heavenlier world than this?
  And if there is
Will the heart of any everlasting thing
  Bring me these dreams that take my breath away?
They come at evening with the home-flying rooks and the scent of hay,
Over the fields. They come in Spring.

In Nunhead Cemetery

It is the clay that makes the earth stick to his spade;
    He fills in holes like this year after year;
The others have gone; they were tired, and half afraid,
    But I would rather be standing here;

There is nowhere else to go. I have seen this place
    From the windows of the train that's going past
Against the sky. This is rain on my face –
    It was raining here when I saw it last.

There is something horrible about a flower;
    This, broken in my hand, is one of those
He threw it in just now; it will not live another hour;
    There are thousands more: you do not miss a rose.

One of the children hanging about
    Pointed at the whole dreadful heap and smiled
This morning after *that* was carried out;
    There is something terrible about a child.

We were like children last week, in the Strand;
    That was the day you laughed at me
Because I tried to make you understand
    The cheap, stale chap I used to be
    Before I saw the things you made me see.

This is not a real place; perhaps by-and-by
    I shall wake – I am getting drenched with all this rain:
To-morrow I will tell you about the eyes of the Crystal Palace train
    Looking down on us, and you will laugh and I shall see what you see again.

    Not here, not now. We said 'Not yet
    Across our low stone parapet
Will the quick shadows of the sparrows fall.'

But still it was a lovely thing
Through the grey months to wait for Spring
With the birds that go a-gypsying
In the parks till the blue seas call.
And next to these, you used to care
For the lions in Trafalgar Square,
Who'll stand and speak for London when her bell of Judgement tolls –
And the gulls at Westminster that were
The old sea-captains' souls.
To-day again the brown tide splashes' step by step, the river stair,
And the gulls are there!

By a month we have missed our Day:
The children would have hung about
Round the carriage and over the way
As you and I came out.

We should have stood on the gulls' black cliffs and heard the sea
And seen the moon's white track,
I would have called, you would have come to me
And kissed me back.

You have never done that: I do not know
Why I stood staring at your bed
And heard you, though you spoke so low,
But could not reach your hands, your little head;
There was nothing we could not do, you said,
And you went, and I let you go!

Now I will burn you back, I will burn you through,
Though I am damned for it we two will lie
And burn, here where the starlings fly
To these white stones from the wet sky – ;
Dear, you will say this is not I –
It would not be you, it would not be you!

If for only a little while
    You will think of it you will understand,
      If you will touch my sleeve and smile
    As you did that morning in the Strand
      I can wait quietly with you
      Or go away if you want me to –
    God! What is God? but your face has gone and your hand!
    Let me stay here too.

    When I was quite a little lad
    At Christmas time we went half mad
      For joy of all the toys we had,
And then we used to sing about the sheep
      The shepherds watched by night;
We used to pray to Christ to keep
      Our small souls safe till morning light – ;
I am scared, I am staying with you to-night –
          Put me to sleep.

I shall stay here: here you can see the sky;
The houses in the streets are much too high;
    There is no one left to speak to there;
    Here they are everywhere,
And just above them fields and fields of roses lie –
If he would dig it all up again they would not die.

Fame

Sometimes in the over-heated house, but not for long,
    Smirking and speaking rather loud,
   I see myself among the crowd,
Where no one fits the singer to his song,
Or sifts the unpainted from the painted faces
Of the people who are always on my stair;
They were not with me when I walked in heavenly places;
    But could I spare
In the blind Earth's great silences and spaces,
   The din, the scuffle, the long stare
    If I went back and it was not there?
Back to the old known things that are the new,
The folded glory of the gorse, the sweetbriar air,
To the larks that cannot praise us, knowing nothing of what we do,
    And the divine, wise trees that do not care.
Yet, to leave Fame, still with such eyes and that bright hair!
God! If I might! And before I go hence
    Take in her stead
    To our tossed bed
One little dream, no matter how small, how wild.
Just now, I think I found it in a field, under a fence –
A frail, dead, new-born lamb, ghostly and pitiful and white
    A blot upon the night,
    The moon's dropped child!

The Quiet House

When we were children old Nurse used to say,
    The house was like an auction or a fair
Until the lot of us were safe in bed.
It has been quiet as the country-side
Since Ted and Janey and then Mother died
And Tom crossed Father and was sent away.
After the lawsuit he could not hold up his head,
    Poor Father, and he does not care
For people here, or to go anywhere.

To get away to Aunt's for that week-end
    Was hard enough; (since then, a year ago,
    He scarcely lets me slip out of his sight –)
At first I did not like my cousin's friend,
    I did not think I should remember him:
    His voice has gone, his face is growing dim
And if I like him now I do not know.
    He frightened me before he smiled –
    He did not ask me if he might –
    He said that he would come one Sunday night,
    He spoke to me as if I were a child.

No year has been like this that has just gone by;
    It may be that what Father says is true,
If things are so it does not matter why:
    But everything has burned, and not quite through.
    The colours of the world have turned
    To flame, the blue, the gold has burned
In what used to be such a leaden sky.
When you are burned quite through you die.

    Red is the strangest pain to bear;
In Spring the leaves on the budding trees;
In Summer the roses are worse than these,
    More terrible than they are sweet:
    A rose can stab you across the street
        Deeper than any knife:

And the crimson haunts you everywhere –
Thin shafts of sunlight, like the ghosts of reddened swords have struck our stair
As if, coming down, you had spilt your life.

   I think that my soul is red
Like the soul of a sword or a scarlet flower:
   But when these are dead
   They have had their hour.

I shall have had mine, too,
   For from head to feet,
I am burned and stabbed half through,
   And the pain is deadly sweet.

The things that kill us seem
   Blind to the death they give:
It is only in our dream
   The things that kill us live.

The room is shut where Mother died,
   The other rooms are as they were,
The world goes on the same outside,
   The sparrows fly across the Square,
   The children play as we four did there,
   The trees grow green and brown and bare,
The sun shines on the dead Church spire,
   And nothing lives here but the fire,
While Father watches from his chair
         Day follows day
The same, or now and then, a different grey,
       Till, like his hair,
Which Mother said was wavy once and bright,
       They will all turn white.

   To-night I heard a bell again –
Outside it was the same mist of fine rain,
The lamps just lighted down the long, dim street,
       No one for me –
   I think it is myself I go to meet:
I do not care; some day I *shall* not think; I shall not *be*!

À quoi bon dire

Seventeen years ago you said
    Something that sounded like Good-bye;
    And everybody thinks that you are dead,
        But I.

So I, as I grow stiff and cold
To this and that say Good-bye too;
    And everybody sees that I am old
        But you.

And one fine morning in a sunny lane
Some boy and girl will meet and kiss and swear
    That nobody can love their way again
        While over there
You will have smiled, I shall have tossed your hair.

Monsieur qui passe

(Quai Voltaire)

A purple blot against the dead white door
In my friend's rooms, bathed in their vile pink light,
I had not noticed her before
She snatched my eyes and threw them back to me:
She did not speak till we came out into the night,
Paused at this bench beside the kiosk on the quay.

God knows precisely what she said –
I left to her the twisted skein,
Though here and there I caught a thread, –
Something, at first, about 'the lamps along the Seine,
And Paris, with that witching card of Spring
Kept up her sleeve, – why you could see
The trick done on these freezing winter nights!
While half the kisses of the Quay –
Youth, hope, – the whole enchanted string
Of dreams hung on the Seine's long line of lights.'

Then suddenly she stripped, the very skin
Came off her soul, – a mere girl clings
Longer to some last rag, however thin,
When she has shown you – well – all sorts of things:
'If it were daylight-oh! one keeps one's head –
But fourteen years! – No one has ever guessed –
The whole thing starts when one gets to bed –
Death? – If the dead would tell us they had rest!
But your eyes held it as I stood there by the door –
One speaks to Christ – one tries to catch His garment's hem –
One hardly says as much to Him – no more:
It was not you, it was your eyes – I spoke to them.'

She stopped like a shot bird that flutters still,
And drops, and tries to run again, and swerves.
The tale should end in some walled house upon a hill.
My eyes, at least, won't play such havoc there, –
Or hers – But she had hair! – blood dipped in gold;
And there she left me throwing back the first odd stare.
Some sort of beauty once, but turning yellow, getting old.
Pouah! These women and their nerves!
God! but the night *is* cold!

Rooms

I remember rooms that have had their part
    In the steady slowing down of the heart.
The room in Paris, the room at Geneva,
The little damp room with the seaweed smell,
And that ceaseless maddening sound of the tide –
    Rooms where for good or for ill – things died.
But there is the room where we two lie dead,
Though every morning we seem to wake and might just as well seem to sleep again
    As we shall somewhere in the other quieter, dustier bed
    Out there in the sun – in the rain.

My Heart is Lame

My heart is lame with running after yours so fast
    Such a long way,
Shall we walk slowly home, looking at all the things we passed
    Perhaps to-day?

Home down the quiet evening roads under the quiet skies,
    Not saying much,
You for a moment giving me your eyes
    When you could bear my touch.

But not to-morrow. This has taken all my breath;
    Then, though you look the same,
There may be something lovelier in Love's face in death
As your heart sees it, running back the way we came;
    My heart is lame.

On the Road to the Sea

We passed each other, turned and stopped for half an hour, then went our way,
    I who make other women smile did not make you –
But no man can move mountains in a day.
    So this hard thing is yet to do.

But first I want your life: – before I die I want to see
    The world that lies behind the strangeness of your eyes,
There is nothing gay or green there for my gathering, it may be,
        Yet on brown fields there lies
A haunting purple bloom: is there not something in grey skies
            And in grey sea?
    I want what world there is behind your eyes,
    I want your life and you will not give it me.

Now, if I look, I see you walking down the years,
    Young, and through August fields – a face, a thought, a swinging dream perched on
                    a stile –
    I would have liked (so vile we are!) to have taught you tears
        But most to have made you smile.

To-day is not enough or yesterday: God sees it all –
Your length on sunny lawns, the wakeful rainy nights – ; tell me – ; (how vain to ask),
                but it is not a question – just a call – ;
Show me then, only your notched inches climbing up the garden wall,
        I like you best when you were small.

    Is this a stupid thing to say
    Not having spent with you one day?
No matter; I shall never touch your hair
Or hear the little tick behind your breast,
    Still it is there,
    And as a flying bird
Brushes the branches where it may not rest
    I have brushed your hand and heard
The child in you: I like that best

So small, so dark, so sweet; and were you also then too grave and wise?
    Always I think. Then put your far off little hand in mine; – Oh! let it rest;
I will not stare into the early world beyond the opening eyes,
    Or vex or scare what I love best.
        But I want your life before mine bleeds away –
        Here – not in heavenly hereafters – soon, –
        I want your smile this very afternoon,
        (The last of all my vices, pleasant people used to say,
        I wanted and I sometimes got – the Moon!)

        You know, at dusk, the last bird's cry,
    And round the house the flap of the bat's low flight,
        Trees that go black against the sky
    And then – how soon the night!

    No shadow of you on any bright road again,
And at the darkening end of this – what voice? whose kiss? As if you'd say!
It is not I who have walked with you, it will not be I who take away
    Peace, peace, my little handful of the gleaner's grain
    From your reaped fields at the shut of day.

    Peace! Would you not rather die
Reeling, – with all the cannons at your ear?
    So, at least, would I,
And I may not be here
To-night, to-morrow morning or next year.
Still I will let you keep your life a little while,
        See dear?
    I have made you smile.

Fin de fête

Sweetheart, for such a day
 One mustn't grudge the score;
Here, then, it's all to pay,
 It's Goodnight at the door.

Goodnight and good dreams to you, –
 Do you remember the picture-book thieves
Who left two children sleep in a wood the long night through,
 And how the birds came down and covered them with leaves?

So you and I should have slept, – But now,
 Oh, what a lonely head!
With just the shadow of a waving bough
 In the moonlight over your head.

The Changeling

Toll no bell for me, dear Father, dear Mother,
    Waste no sighs;
There are my sisters, there is my little brother
  Who plays in the place called Paradise,
Your children all, your children for ever;
        But I, so wild,
Your disgrace, with the queer brown face, was never,
  Never, I know, but half your child!

In the garden at play, all day, last summer,
    Far and away I heard
The sweet 'tweet-tweet' of a strange new-comer,
  The dearest, clearest call of a bird.
It lived down there in the deep green hollow,
  My own old home, and the fairies say
The word of a bird is a thing to follow,
  So I was away a night and a day.

One evening, too, by the nursery fire,
  We snuggled close and sat round so still,
When suddenly as the wind blew higher,
  Something scratched on the window-sill,
A pinched brown face peered in – I shivered;
  No one listened or seemed to see;
The arms of it waved and the wings of it quivered,
  Whoo – I knew it had come for me!
  Some are as bad as bad can be!
All night long they danced in the rain,
Round and round in a dripping chain,
Threw their caps at the window-pane,
  Tried to make me scream and shout
  And fling the bedclothes all about:
I meant to stay in bed that night,
And if only you had left a light
  They would never have got me out.

Sometimes I wouldn't speak, you see,
  Or answer when you spoke to me,
Because in the long, still dusks of Spring
You can hear the whole world whispering;
  The shy green grasses making love,
  The feathers grow on the dear, grey dove,
  The tiny heart of the redstart beat,
  The patter of the squirrel's feet,
The pebbles pushing in the silver streams,
The rushes talking in their dreams,
  The swish-swish of the bat's black wings,
  The wild-wood bluebell's sweet ting-tings,
    Humming and hammering at your ear,
    Everything there is to hear
In the heart of hidden things,
  But not in the midst of the nursery riot,
  That's why I wanted to be quiet,
      Couldn't do my sums, or sing,
      Or settle down to anything.
  And when, for that, I was sent upstairs
  I *did* kneel down to say my prayers;
But the King who sits on your high church steeple
Has nothing to do with us fairy people!

Times I pleased you, dear Father, dear Mother,
  Learned all my lessons and liked to play,
And dearly I loved the little pale brother
  Whom some other bird must have called away.
Why did They bring me here to make me
  Not quite bad and not quite good,
Why, unless They're wicked, do They want, in spite, to take me
  Back to Their wet, wild wood?
Now, every night I shall see the windows shining,
  The gold lamp's glow, and the fire's red gleam,
While the best of us are twining twigs and the rest of us are whining
      In the hollow by the stream.
Black and chill are Their nights on the wold;
  And They live so long and They feel no pain:
I shall grow up, but never grow old,
I shall always, always be very cold,
    I shall never come back again!

The Cenotaph

Not yet will those measureless fields be green again
Where only yesterday the wild, sweet, blood of wonderful youth was shed;
There is a grave whose earth must hold too long, too deep a stain,
Though for ever over it we may speak as proudly as we may tread.
But here, where the watchers by lonely hearths from the thrust of an inward sword have
more slowly bled,
We shall build the Cenotaph: Victory, winged, with Peace, winged too, at the column's
head.
And over the stairway, at the foot – oh! here, leave desolate, passionate hands to spread
Violets, roses, and laurel, with the small, sweet, tinkling country things
Speaking so wistfully of other Springs,
From the little gardens of little places where son or sweetheart was born and bred.
In splendid sleep, with a thousand brothers,
        To lovers – to mothers
        Here, too, lies he:
Under the purple, the green, the red,
It is all young life: it must break some women's heart to see
Such a brave, gay coverlet to such a bed!
Only, when all is done and said,
God is not mocked and neither are the dead
For this will stand in our Marketplace –
        Who'll sell, who'll buy
        (Will you or I
Lie each to each with the better grace)?
While looking into every busy whore's and huckster's face
As they drive their bargains, is the Face
Of God: and some young, piteous, murdered face.

I so liked Spring

I so liked Spring last year
   Because you were here; –
     The thrushes too –
Because it was these you so liked to hear –
     I so liked you.

   This year's a different thing, –
     I'll not think of you.
But I'll like the Spring because it is simply Spring
     As the thrushes do.

The Forest Road

The forest road,
The infinite straight road stretching away
World without end: the breathless road between the walls
Of the black listening trees: the hushed, grey road
Beyond the window that you shut to-night
Crying that you would look at it by day –
There is a shadow there that sings and calls
But not for you. Oh! hidden eyes that plead in sleep
Against the lonely dark, if I could touch the fear
And leave it kissed away on quiet lids –
If I could hush these hands that are half-awake,
Groping for me in sleep I could go free.
I wish that God would take them out of mine
And fold them like the wings of frightened birds
Shot cruelly down, but fluttering into quietness so soon.
Broken, forgotten things; there is no grief for them in the green Spring
When the new birds fly back to the old trees.
But it shall not be so with you. I will look back. I wish I knew that God would stand
Smiling and looking down on you when morning comes,
To hold you, when you wake, closer than I,
So gently though: and not with famished lips or hungry arms:
He does not hurt the frailest, dearest things
As we do in the dark. See, dear, your hair –
I must unloose this hair that sleeps and dreams
About my face, and clings like the brown weed
To drowned, delivered things, tossed by the tired sea
Back to the beaches. Oh! your hair! If you had lain
A long time dead on the rough, glistening ledge
Of some black cliff, forgotten by the tide,
The raving winds would tear, the dripping brine would rust away
Fold after fold of all the loveliness
That wraps you round, and makes you, lying here,
The passionate fragrance that the roses are.
But death would spare the glory of your head
In the long sweetness of the hair that does not die:
The spray would leap to it in every storm,
The scent of the unsilenced sea would linger on

In these dark waves, and round the silence that was you –
Only the nesting gulls would hear – but there would still be whispers in your hair;
Keep them for me; keep them for me. What is this singing on the road
That makes all other music like the music in a dream –
Dumb to the dancing and the marching feet; you know, in dreams, you see
Old pipers playing that you cannot hear,
And ghostly drums that only seem to beat. This seems to climb:
Is it the music of a larger place? It makes our room too small: it is like a stair,
A calling stair that climbs up to a smile you scarcely see,
Dim, but so waited for; and *you* know what a smile is, how it calls,
How if I smiled you always ran to me.
Now you must sleep forgetfully, as children do.
There is a Spirit sits by us in sleep
Nearer than those who walk with us in the bright day.
I think he has a tranquil, saving face: I think he came
Straight from the hills: he may have suffered there in time gone by,
And once, from those forsaken heights, looked down,
Lonely himself, on all the lonely sorrows of the earth.
It is his kingdom – Sleep. If I could leave you there –
If, without waking you, I could get up and reach the door –!
We used to go together. – Shut, scared eyes,
Poor, desolate, desperate hands, it is not I
Who thrust you off. No, take your hands away –
I cannot strike your lonely hands. Yes, I have struck your heart,
It did not come so near. Then lie you there
Dear and wild heart behind this quivering snow
With two red stains on it: and I will strike and tear
Mine out, and scatter it to yours. Oh! throbbing dust,
You that were life, our little wind-blown hearts!
                    The road! the road!
There is a shadow there: I see my soul,
I hear my soul, singing among the trees!

The Shade-Catchers

I think they are about as high
      As haycocks are. They went running by
Catching bits of shade in the sunny street:
'I've got one,' cried sister to brother.
      'I've got two.' 'Now I've got another.'
But scudding away on their little bare feet
They left the shade in the sunny street.

From a Window

Up here, with June, the sycamore throws
    Across the window a whispering screen;
I shall miss the sycamore more, I suppose,
Than anything else on this earth that is out in green.
  But I mean to go through the door without fear,
  Not caring much what happens here
    When I'm away: –
How green the screen is across the panes
  Or who goes laughing along the lanes
With my old lover all the summer day.

The Trees are Down

– and he cried with a loud voice:
Hurt not the earth, neither the sea, nor the trees –

Revelation

They are cutting down the great plane-trees at the end of the gardens.
For days there has been the grate of the saw, the swish of the branches as they fall,
The crash of trunks, the rustle of trodden leaves,
With the 'Whoops' and the 'Whoas', the loud common talk, the loud common laughs of
the men, above it all.

I remember one evening of a long past Spring
Turning in at a gate, getting out of a cart, and finding a large dead rat in the mud of the
drive.
I remember thinking: alive or dead, a rat was a god-forsaken thing,
But at least, in May, that even a rat should be alive.

The week's work here is as good as done. There is just one bough
    On the roped bole, in the fine grey rain,
        Green and high
        And lonely against the sky.
            (Down now! –)
        And but for that,
        If an old dead rat
Did once, for a moment, unmake the Spring, I might never have thought of him again.

It is not for a moment the Spring is unmade to-day;
These were great trees, it was in them from root to stem:
When the men with the 'Whoops' and the 'Whoas' have carted the whole of the
whispering loveliness away
Half the Spring, for me, will have gone with them.

It is going now, and my heart has been struck with the hearts of the planes;
Half my life it has beat with these, in the sun, in the rains,
    In the March wind, the May breeze,
In the great gales that came over to them across the roofs from the great seas.
    There was only a quiet rain when they were dying;
    They must have heard the sparrows flying,

And the small creeping creatures in the earth where they were lying –
But I, all day, I heard an angel crying:
'Hurt not the trees.'

A Farewell

Remember me and smile, as smiling too,
    I have remembered things that went their way –
    The dolls with which I grew too wise to play –
Or over-wise – and kissed, as children do,
And so dismissed them; yes, even as you
    Have done with this poor piece of painted clay –
    Not wantonly, but wisely, shall we say?
As one who, haply, tunes his heart anew.

Only I wish her eyes may not be blue,
    The eyes of a new angel. Ah! she may
Miss something that I found, – perhaps the clue
To those long silences of yours, which grew
    Into one word. And should she not be gay,
    Poor lady! Well, she too must have her day!

I Have Been Through the Gates

His heart to me, was a place of palaces and pinnacles and shining towers;
I saw it then as we see things in dreams, – I do not remember how long I slept;
I remember the trees, and the high, white walls, and how the sun was always on the
                                                             towers;
The walls are standing to-day, and the gates: I have been through the gates, I have
                                               groped, I have crept
Back, back. There is dust in the streets, and blood; they are empty; darkness is over them;
His heart is a place with the lights gone out, forsaken by great winds and the heavenly
                                        rain, unclean and unswept,
Like the heart of the holy city, old, blind, beautiful Jerusalem,
           Over which Christ wept.

Madeleine in Church

Here, in the darkness where this plaster saint
    Stands nearer than God stands to our distress,
And one small candle shines, but not so faint
    As the far lights of everlastingness,
I'd rather kneel than over there, in open day
    Where Christ is hanging, rather pray
      To something more like my own clay,
        Not too divine;
      For once, perhaps, my little saint
      Before he got his niche and crown,
Had one short stroll about the town;
It brings him closer, just that taint
      And anyone can wash the paint
Off our poor faces, his and mine!

Is that why I see Monty now? equal to any saint, poor boy, as good as gold,
But still, with just the proper trace
Of earthliness on his shining wedding face;
And then gone suddenly blank and old
The hateful day of the divorce:
Stuart got his, hands down, of course
Crowing like twenty cocks and grinning like a horse:
But Monty took it hard. All said and done, I liked him best, –
He was the first, he stands out clearer than the rest.
      It seems so funny all we other rips
    Should have immortal souls; Monty and Redge quite damnably
Keep theirs afloat while we go down like scuttled ships, –
      It's funny too, how easily we sink,
        One might put up a monument, I think
   To half the world and cut across it 'Lost at Sea!'
I should drown Jim, poor little sparrow, if I netted him to-night –
      No, it's no use this penny light –
    Or my poor saint with his tin-pot crown –
    The trees of Calvary are where they were,
      When we are sure that we can spare
   The tallest, let us go and strike it down
And leave the other two still standing there.

I too would ask him to remember me
If there were any Paradise beyond this earth that I could see.

Oh! quiet Christ who never knew
The poisonous fangs that bite us through
And make us do the things we do,
See how we suffer and fight and die,
How helpless and how low we lie,
God holds You and You hang so high,
Though no one looking long at You,
Can think You do not suffer too,
But, up there, from your still, star-lighted tree
What can You know, what can You really see
Of this dark ditch, the soul of me!

We are what we are: when I was half a child I could not sit
Watching black shadows on green lawns and red carnations burning in the sun,
Without paying so heavily for it
That joy and pain, like any mother and her unborn child were almost one.
I could hardly bear
The dreams upon the eyes of white geraniums in the dusk,
The thick, close voice of musk,
The jessamine music on the thin night air,
Or, sometimes, my own hands about me anywhere –
The sight of my own face (for it was lovely then) even the scent of my own hair,
Oh! there was nothing, nothing that did not sweep to the high seat
Of laughing gods, and then blow down and beat
My soul into the highway dust, as hoofs do the dropped roses of the street.
I think my body was my soul,
And when we are made thus
Who shall control
Our hands, our eyes, the wandering passion of our feet,
Who shall teach us
To thrust the world out of our heart; to say, till perhaps in death,
When the race is run,
And it is forced from us with our last breath
'Thy will be done'?
If it is Your will that we should be content with the tame, bloodless things,
As pale as angels smirking by, with folded wings.
Oh! I know Virtue and the peace it brings!

The temperate, well-worn smile
The one man gives you, when you are evermore his own:
And afterwards the child's, for a little while,
With its unknowing and all-seeing eyes
So soon to change, and make you feel how quick
The clock goes round. If one had learned the trick –
(How does one though?) quite early on,
Of long green pastures under placid skies,
One might be walking now with patient truth.
What did we ever care for it, who have asked for youth,
When, oh! my God! this is going or has gone?

There is a portrait of my mother, at nineteen,
With the black spaniel, standing by the garden seat,
The dainty head held high against the painted green
And throwing out the youngest smile, shy, but half haughty and half sweet.
Her picture then: but simply Youth, or simply Spring
To me to-day: a radiance on the wall,
So exquisite, so heart-breaking a thing
Beside the mask that I remember, shrunk and small,
Sapless and lined like a dead leaf,
All that was left of oh! the loveliest face, by time and grief!

And in the glass, last night I saw a ghost behind my chair –
Yet why remember it, when one can still go moderately gay – ?
Or could – with any one of the old crew,
But oh! these boys! the solemn way
They take you, and the things they say –
This 'I have only as long as you'
When you remind them you are not precisely twenty-two –
Although at heart perhaps – God! if it were
Only the face, only the hair!
If Jim had written to me as he did to-day
A year ago – and now it leaves me cold –
I know what this means, old, old, *old*!
Et avec ça – mais on a vécu, tout se paie.

That is not always true: there was my Mother – (well at least the dead are free!)
  Yoked to the man that Father was; yoked to the woman I am, Monty too;
  The little portress at the Convent School, stewing in hell so patiently;
The poor, fair boy who shot himself at Aix. And what of me – and what of me?
  But I, I paid for what I had, and they for nothing. No, one cannot see
    How it shall be made up to them in some serene eternity.
If there were fifty Heavens God could not give us back the child who went or never came;
  Here, on our little patch of this great earth, the sun of any darkened day,
  Not one of all the starry buds hung on the hawthorn trees of last year's May,
    No shadow from the sloping fields of yesterday;
  For every hour they slant across the hedge a different way,
      The shadows are never the same.

      'Find rest in Him!' One knows the parson's tags –
  Back to the fold, across the evening fields, like any flock of baa-ing sheep:
Yes, it may be, when He was shorn, led us to slaughter, torn the bleating soul in us to rags,
      For so he giveth His belovèd sleep.
      Oh! He will take us stripped and done,
      Driven into his heart. So we are won:
  Then safe, safe are we? in the shelter of His everlasting wings –
I do not envy Him His victories. His arms are full of broken things.

      But I shall not be in them. Let Him take
      The finer ones, the easier to break.
And they are not gone, yet, for me, the lights, the colours, the perfumes.
      Though now they speak rather in sumptuous rooms
        In silks and in gem-like wines;
    Here, even, in this corner where my little candle shines
        And overhead the lancet-window glows
        With golds and crimsons you could almost drink
To know how jewels taste, just as I used to think
There was a scent in every red and yellow rose
        Of all the sunsets. But this place is grey,
        And much too quiet. No one here,
        Why, this is awful, this is fear!
          Nothing to see, no face,
    Nothing to hear except your heart beating in space
        As if the world was ended. Dead at last!
        Dead soul, dead body, tied together fast.

These to go on with and alone, to the slow end:
No one to sit with, really, or speak to, friend to friend:
Out of the long procession, black or white or red
Not one left now to say 'Still I am here, then see you, dear, lay here your head.'
Only the doll's house looking on the Park
To-night, all nights, I know, when the man puts the lights out, very dark.
With upstairs, in the blue and gold box of a room, just the maids' footsteps overhead,
Then utter silence and the empty world –the room – the bed –
The corpse! No, not quite dead, while this cries out in me,
But nearly: very soon to be
A handful of forgotten dust –
There must be someone. Christ! there must,
Tell me there *will* be someone. Who?
If there were no one else, could it be You?

How old was Mary out of whom you cast
So many devils? Was she young or perhaps for years
She had sat staring, with dry eyes, at this and that man going past
Till suddenly she saw You on the steps of Simon's house
And stood and looked at You through tears.
I think she must have known by those
The thing, for what it was that had come to her.
For some of us there is a passion, I suppose
So far from earthly cares and earthly fears
That in its stillness you can hardly stir
Or in its nearness, lift your hand,
So great that you have simply got to stand
Looking at it through tears, through tears.
Then straight from these there broke the kiss,
I think You must have known by this
The thing for what it was, that had come to You:
She did not love You like the rest,
It was in her own way, but at the worst, the best,
She gave you something altogether new.
And through it all, from her, no word.
She scarcely saw You, scarcely heard:
Surely You knew when she so touched You with her hair,
Or by the wet cheek lying there,
And while her perfume clung to You from head to feet all through the day
That You can change the things for which we care,
But even You, unless You kill us, not the way.

This, then was peace for her, but passion too.
I wonder was it like a kiss that once I knew,
The only one that I would care to take
Into the grave with me, to which if there were afterwards, to wake.
Almost as happy as the carven dead
In some dim chancel lying head by head
We slept with it, but face to face, the whole night through –
One breath, one throbbing quietness, as if the thing behind our lips was endless life,
Lost, as I woke, to hear in the strange earthly dawn, his 'Are you there?'
And lie still, listening to the wind outside, among the firs.

So, Mary, chose the dream of Him for what was left to her of night and day,
It is the only truth: it is the dream in us that neither life nor death nor any other thing
can take away:
But if she had not touched Him in the doorway of the dream could she have cared so
much?
She was a sinner, we are what we are: the spirit afterwards, but first, the touch.
And He has never shared with me my haunted house beneath the trees
Of Eden and Calvary, with its ghosts that have not any eyes for tears,
And the happy guests who would not see, or if they did, remember these,
Though they lived there a thousand years.
Outside, too gravely looking at me, He seems to stand,
And looking at Him, if my forgotten spirit came
Unwillingly back, what could it claim
Of those calm eyes, that quiet speech,
Breaking like a slow tide upon the beach,
The scarred, not quiet human hand?
Unwillingly back to the burden of old imaginings
When it has learned so long not to think, not to be,
Again, again it would speak as it has been spoken to me of things
That I shall not see!

I cannot bear to look at this divinely bent and gracious head:
When I was small I never quite believed that He was dead:
And at the Convent school I used to lie awake in bed
Thinking about His hands. It did not matter what they said,
He was alive to me, so hurt, so hurt! And most of all in Holy Week
When there was no one else to see
I used to think it would not hurt me too, so terribly,
If He had ever seemed to notice me
Or if, for once, He would only speak.

Not for that City

Not for that city of the level sun,
      Its golden streets and glittering gates ablaze –
      The shadeless, sleepless city of white days,
White nights, or nights and days that are as one –
We weary, when all is said, all thought, all done.
      We strain our eyes beyond this dusk to see
      What, from the threshold of eternity
We shall step into. No, I think we shun
The splendour of that everlasting glare,
      The clamour of that never-ending song.
      And if for anything we greatly long,
It is for some remote and quiet stair
      Which winds to silence and a space of sleep
      Too sound for waking, and for dreams too deep.

Pêri en mer

Cameret

One day the friends who stand about my bed
    Will slowly turn from it to speak of me
Indulgently, as of the newly dead,
    Not knowing how I perished by the sea,
That night in summer when the gulls topped white
    The crowded masts cut black against a sky
Of fading rose —where suddenly the light
    Of Youth went out and I, no longer I,
Climbed home, the homeless ghost I was to be.
    Yet as I passed they sped me up the heights —
Old seamen round the door of the Abrí
    De la Tempête. Even on quiet nights
    So may some ship go down with all her lights
Beyond the sight of watchers on the quay!

Bishop, J. Dean. 'Ascent into Nothingness: The Poetry of Charlotte Mew'. Dissertation, Louisiana State University, 1968

Davidow, Mary C. 'Charlotte Mew: Biography and Criticism'. Ph.D. thesis, Brown University, 1960

Fitzgerald, Penelope. *Charlotte Mew and Her Friends: with a selection of her poems.* Forward by Brad Leithauser (Addison-Wesley, Reading MA 1988)

Mew, Charlotte. *Collected Poems and Prose* ed. Val Warner (Carcanet Press in association with Virago Press, Manchester and London 1982; revised edn *Collected Poems and Selected Prose*, Carcanet Press, Manchester 1997, 2003)

— *The Farmer's Bride* (The Poetry Bookshop, London 1916)

— *The Rambling Sailor* (The Poetry Bookshop, London 1929)

— *Saturday Market* (Macmillan, New York 1921)

— *Selected Poems* ed. Ian Hamilton (Bloomsbury, London 1999)

Monro, Alida. 'Charlotte Mew: A Memoir' (preface to *Collected Poems of Charlotte Mew*, London, Duckworth 1953)

— 'Charlotte Mew' (a critical note on her poetry, *The Chapbook*, June 1920)

Parris, P.B. *His Arms are Full of Broken Things* (a fictionalised biography of Mew, London, Viking 1997)

Swinnerton, Frank. 'Charlotte Mew', *The Georgian Literary Scene 1910–1935* (London, Heinemann 1935), p. 251

Watts, Marjorie. 'Memories of Charlotte Mew', *PEN Broadsheet* 13 (Autumn 1982), pp.12–13

Index of First Lines

Index of Titles

Fyfield*Books*

Two millennia of essential classics
The extensive Fyfield*Books* list includes

For more information, including a full list of Fyfield*Books* and a contents list for each title, and details of how to order the books, visit the Carcanet website at www.carcanet.co.uk or email info@carcanet.co.uk